STITCH IT FOR
Spring

Lynette Anderson

D&C

David and Charles

www.stitchcraftcreate.co.uk

Contents

Introduction

Spring for me is the promise of things to come, a riot of colour arriving after a bare, wintery world. I love the buds that first appear, watching as they get fatter and fatter with colours that cannot wait to burst out and show themselves, either in the blossom on the trees or the bulbs from the earth.

It was with great delight that I drew and stitched the projects in this book, drawing on my childhood memories and using fabrics from my 'Wildflower Wood' fabric collection. As a child I lived in the country and played with my brother in the woods near our home. I loved learning the flower names from my mother and made friends with the wild creatures that lived there. I remember planting daffodils with my mother along the edge of the driveway to our country home and trying to be patient while I waited for the seasons to pass until it was time for them to burst into life. If the season is right when I drive past my childhood home I look for those daffodils we planted together so long ago.

The projects in this book are both practical and decorative, combining patchwork, appliqué and decorative stitching in charming designs. You can choose from a range of lovely ideas for your home: perhaps the delightful Birdhouse Blossoms Picture or the gorgeous Garden Delights Table Centre or the Spring Flower Quilt. If you are seeking quick little gifts for friends and family the Night Owl Purse, the Night and Day Charms and the Sweet Rabbit Tea Towel may be just what you are looking for. And why not make something just for yourself? The Dreaming Tree Journal and the stylish Hexagon Handbag are bound to be much admired.

Whatever you chose to make, my wish is for you to enjoy stitching the projects within this book, and that your family will enjoy them for many years to come.

Dedication
Mum, thank you for teaching me the names of the birds and flowers when I was a child and for all the encouragement through the years.

General Techniques

This section describes the basic techniques you will need to make and finish off the projects in this book, from transferring designs to binding a finished quilt. Beginners should find it very useful.

Sewing and Pressing

Patchwork or pieced work requires accurate seams. For really accurate piecing sew a *bare* ¼in (6mm) seam, as this will allow for thread thickness and the tiny amount of fabric taken up when the seam is pressed.

Generally, press seams towards the darker fabric to avoid dark colours showing through on the right side. Press joining seams in opposite directions so they lock together and make the flattest join. Press (don't iron) and be careful with steam as this can stretch fabric.

Joining Strips

Sometimes fabric strips need to be joined together for borders or binding. Joining them with a diagonal seam at a 45-degree angle will make them less noticeable, as will pressing the seams open (Fig 1).

Fig 1

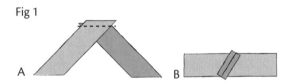

A   B

Making Bias Binding

Bias binding is made from fabric strips cut on the cross grain (bias) direction of the fabric, which makes the strips more flexible.

one Fold the fabric in half diagonally and crease lightly. Open out and cut strips 1¼in (3.2cm) wide diagonally across the fabric. Join the strips to the length required.

two Fold and press about ¼in (6mm) of fabric towards the wrong side along the entire length.

Using Templates

The project templates are given full size in the Template section. Trace the template on to paper or thin card, cut out and use as a pattern to cut the shape from paper. Before cutting out check whether a ¼in (6mm) seam allowance is needed, which it will be if using a needle-turn appliqué technique.

Reversing templates

Templates being used for fusible web appliqué will need to be reversed (flipped). You could place a copy of the template on to a light source with the template right side down rather than up and trace it this way. You could also trace the template on to tracing paper, turn the tracing paper over and trace the template again on to paper.

Transferring designs

Designs can be transferred on to fabric in various ways. I use a light source, such as a light box, a window or a light under a glass table. Iron your fabric so it is free of creases. Place the design right side up and then the fabric right side up on top, taping it in place. Use a fine-tipped fabric marking pen or a pencil to trace the design. If the marks might show later then use an erasable marker, such as an air-erasable or water-soluble one.

English Paper Piecing

This type of patchwork is also called English patchwork and uses templates, usually made of paper or thin card. Fabric pieces are wrapped around the template and tacked (basted) to it. The patches are then hand sewn together and the papers removed.

one From a master template, create enough paper templates for the project. When cutting out the fabric pieces you need to allow for a ¼in (6mm) seam all round. Make one master template but this time add a ¼in (6mm) seam allowance all round and use this to cut out your fabric pieces.

two Follow Figs 2A–D and pin a paper template to a fabric shape and fold the seam allowance over the edges of the template, tacking (basting) in place through all layers. Keep the fabric firm around the paper shape and tuck in all points neatly. Repeat with all the fabric pieces.

three Place two fabric shapes right sides together, aligning edges and use small whip stitches to sew them together through the folded fabric but not through the paper (Fig 2E). Place a third fabric shape right sides together with the second and sew together. Continue building the design in this way. Once all stitching is finished remove the tacking and the papers.

Making Yoyos

Yoyos are sometimes called Suffolk puffs. They are really easy to make and add a lovely three-dimensional touch to patchwork and appliqué.

one Using a fine-tipped pencil or fabric marking pen, draw around a circular template on the wrong side of your fabrics. Cut out on the line (the seam allowance is included in the project template).

two Thread your needle with a double strand of sewing cotton and knot one end. Take one of the circles and with wrong side facing you fold over about ¼in (6mm). Make a running stitch around the edge (see Fig 3A), turning the ¼in (6mm) in as you go.

three When back to where you started, gently pull on the thread to gather it. Wriggle the yoyo between your fingers to get it into shape (Fig 3B). Pull the thread firmly and tie off the thread off at the back and bury the ends inside the yoyo.

Fig 3

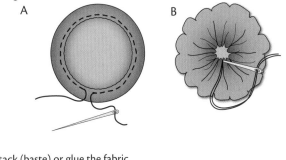

Fig 2

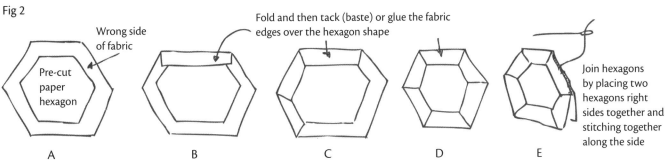

Appliqué Methods

Appliqué is the technique of fixing one fabric shape or pattern on top of another, and can be done in various ways. I have used two methods for the projects in this book – needle-turn appliqué and fusible web appliqué. You may also like to use an appliqué mat.

Needle-turn method

This is a traditional method of hand appliqué where each appliqué piece has a seam turned under all round and is stitched into position on the background fabric. The appliqué shapes may be drawn freehand or templates used, as I have done for the designs in this book.

one Mark the appliqué shape on the right side of your fabric and then mark another line further out all round for the seam allowance. This is usually ¼in (6mm) but may change depending on the size of the appliqué piece being stitched and type of fabric being used. Smaller pieces may only need a ⅛in (3mm) allowance to reduce bulk. Clip the seam allowance on concave curves (the inward ones) to make it easier to turn the seam under.

two For each appliqué piece turn the seam allowance under all round and press. Position the appliqué on the background fabric and stitch into place with tiny slip stitches all round. Press when finished. Some people like to use the needle to turn the seam under as they stitch the appliqué in place.

Fusible web method

Fusible web has an adhesive that melts when heated so when the web is placed between two fabrics the heat of an iron causes the fabrics to fuse together, which makes it ideal for appliqué.

one When using templates for fusible web appliqué they need to be flipped or reversed because you will be drawing the shape on the back of the fabric – see Reversing Templates. Trace around each template on to the paper side of the fusible web, leaving about ½in (1.3cm) around each shape. Cut out roughly around

each shape. Iron the fusible web, paper side up, on to the wrong side of the appliqué fabric and then cut out accurately on your drawn line.

two When the fusible web is cool, peel off the backing paper and place the appliqué in position on your project, right side up. (Check with the template to see which pieces need to go under other pieces, shown by dotted lines on the pattern.) Fuse into place with a medium-hot iron for about ten seconds. Allow the appliqué to cool.

three The edge of the appliqué can be secured further by stitches. I normally use blanket stitch as I like the hand-crafted look but machine satin stitch can also be used.

Making a Quilt Sandwich

A quilt sandwich is a term often used to describe the three layers of a quilt – the top, the wadding (batting) and the backing.

one Press your backing fabric and hang out your wadding to reduce creases. Cut out your wadding and backing about 4in (10.2cm) larger all round than the quilt top. Prepare the quilt top by cutting off or tying in stray ends, pressing it and pressing seam allowances so they lay as flat as possible.

two Lay the backing fabric right side down on a flat surface and tape the corners to keep it flat. Put the wadding on top, smoothing out wrinkles. Now put the quilt top right side up on top.

three Secure the three layers together by using pins or safety pins, tacking (basting) or spray glue. If using pins or tacking, use a grid pattern spacing the lines out about 3in–6in (7.6cm–15.2cm) apart. The sandwich is now ready for quilting.

Quilting

Quilting adds texture and interest to a quilt and secures all the layers together. I have used a combination of hand and machine quilting on the projects in this book. When starting and finishing hand or machine quilting, the starting knot and the thread end need to be hidden in the wadding (batting).

If you need to mark a quilting design on your top this can be done before or after you have made the quilt sandwich. There are many marking pens and pencils available but test them on scrap fabric first. If you are machine quilting, marking lines are more easily covered up. For hand quilting you might prefer to use a removable marker or a light pencil. Some water-erasable markers are set by the heat of an iron so take care when pressing the work.

Binding

Binding a quilt creates a neat and secure edge. A double-fold binding is more durable.

one Measure your completed quilt top around all edges and add about 8in (20.3cm) extra. Cut 2½in (6.3cm) wide strips and join them all together to make the length needed. Fold the binding in half along the length and press.

two Start midway along one side of the quilt and pin the binding along the edge, aligning raw edges. Stitch the binding to the quilt through all layers using a ¼in (6mm) seam until you reach a corner when you should stop ¼in (6mm) away from the end (Fig 4A).

three Remove the work from the machine and fold the binding up, northwards, so it is aligned straight with the edge of the quilt (Fig 4B).

four Hold the corner and fold the binding back down, southwards, aligning it with the raw edge and with the folded corner square. Pin in position and begin sewing again, from the top and over the fold, continuing down the next edge (Fig 4C). Repeat with the other corners.

five When you are nearing the starting point stop 6in (15.2cm) away. Fold back the beginning and end of the binding, so they touch and mark these folds with a pin. Cut the binding ¼in (6mm) from the pin, open out the binding and join with a ¼in (6mm) seam. Press the seam open, re-fold it and slipstitch in place.

six Now fold the binding over to the back of the quilt and slipstitch it in place. Fold the mitres at the corner neatly and secure with tiny slipstitches.

Fig 2

A

B

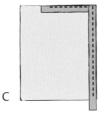

C

Embroidery Stitches

I have used various stitches to create the stitcheries on the projects in this book. I used Cosmo stranded embroidery threads but DMC equivalents are given here. The stitches are all easy to work and fun to do – just follow the simple diagrams.

Embroidery Threads

The projects in this book use Cosmo stranded embroidery threads but DMC alternatives have been provided here.

Cosmo code	Colour	DMC code
235	dusky pink	3726
245	red	815
312	dark brown	838
364	cream	712
368	light brown	3790
575	gold	3829
734	blue	930
763	light mauve	3041
895	charcoal	844
925	green	3011

Blanket stitch

Blanket stitch can be used to edge appliqué motifs and stitched in a circle for flowers. Start at the edge of the appliqué shape, taking the needle through to the back of work and up through to the front of the shape that you are appliquéing a small distance in from the edge where you started (A). Pull the thread through to form a loop (B). Put your needle through the loop from front to back, making sure the loop is not twisted. As you pull the thread into place lift the stitch slightly so that it sits on top of the raw edge rather than sliding underneath (C). Pull the thread firmly into place to avoid loose, floppy stitches. Continue on to make the next stitch (D).

A
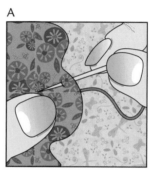

B
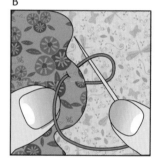

C
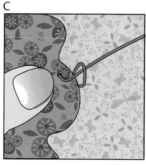

D
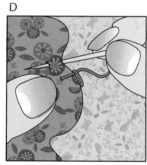

Backstitch

Backstitch is an outlining stitch that I also use to 'draw' parts of the design. It is really easy to work and can follow any parts of a design you choose.

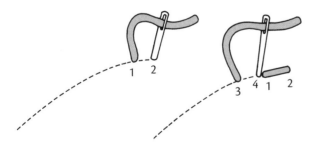

Chain stitch

This stitch can be worked in straight or curved lines for stems and as a single detached stitch.

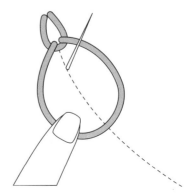

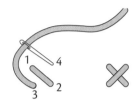

Cross stitch

A simple cross stitch can be used to add pattern to stitcheries, particularly on animal coats.

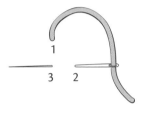
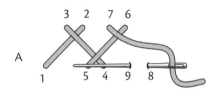
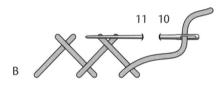

Herringbone stitch

This embroidery stitch is used as a decorative stitch and also a joining stitch on the Night and Day Charms.

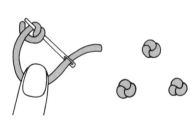

French knot

These little knots are easy to form and are useful for eyes and other details.

Lazy daisy stitch

This decorative stitch is great for flowers especially if the stitches are worked in a circle.

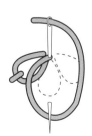

Long stitch

Long stitch is just a single long stitch. It is useful for coat markings, cat's whiskers and so on.

Running stitch

These are evenly spaced stitches that can run in any direction or pattern you choose. Quilting stitch is a running stitch.

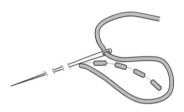
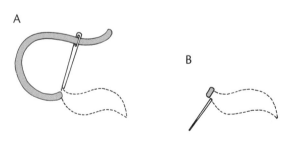

Satin stitch

This stitch is used to fill in areas of a design with long stitches worked side by side.

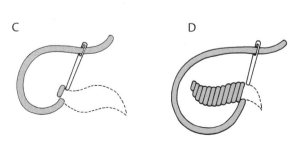

Birdhouse Blossoms Picture

Spring is definitely in the air: the blossom is just showing on the trees, the daisies are in the grass. A simple white frame sets this sweet spring garden scene off to perfection. Add a lovely hand-painted bluebird button and some printed dragonfly ribbon and this little picture will make everyone happy.

Finished size: 6in (16cm) diameter approximately, excluding frame.

What You Will Need

❋ 10in (25cm) square of striped yarn dye for background

❋ 2in (5cm) square each of dusky pink and dusky mauve for birdhouse appliqué

❋ 1in x 2in (2.5cm x 5cm) each of two prints for roof appliqués and brown for poles

❋ Cosmo stranded embroidery threads: 235 pink, 312 dark brown, 364 cream, 575 gold, 734 blue, 763 light mauve, 895 charcoal and 925 green (see General Techniques: Embroidery Threads for DMC alternatives)

❋ 10in (25cm) square stitchery stabilizer

❋ 8in (20.3cm) square of cotton wadding (batting)

❋ Printed dragonfly ribbon (or similar) ⅜in (1cm) wide x 20cm (8in)

❋ Buttons: one bluebird and one tiny pink heart (see Suppliers)

❋ Fine-tipped fabric marking pen

❋ Hot glue gun with glue

❋ Roxanne's Glue Baste It ™ (optional)

❋ Round wooden frame to fit (ideally with removable insert at the back)

Transferring the Design

one Use the templates provided. Using a light source such as a light box or a window, place the striped background fabric right side up and centrally over the stitchery design and trace the design using a fine-tipped fabric marking pen.

two If using an iron-on stitchery stabilizer, iron it on before starting the stitching to avoid thread shadows from showing through on the front of the work. Place the shiny side of the stabilizer on to the wrong side of your fabric and follow the manufacturer's instructions to bond it in place.

Working the Appliqué

three You can do the appliqué before or after the stitchery has been completed – I do mine before. Using your favourite method of appliqué, apply the birdhouses, roofs and poles. See General Techniques: Appliqué Methods. If using needle-turn appliqué (as I did) you will need to add seam allowance to the shapes. I made paper templates for the appliqué shapes and drew around the templates onto the wrong side of my chosen fabrics. I

cut the pieces out, adding a small seam allowance, and turned the seam allowance under all round.

four Stitch the appliqué shapes in position using a blind hem stitch and thread that matches the background fabric so it doesn't show. Press the finished appliqués, first on the wrong side and then on the right side.

five Using a fine-tipped fabric marking pen transfer the surface stitchery lines for the nesting holes and perches on the birdhouses either freehand or using a light box. Position and stitch the ribbon in place.

Working the Stitchery

six Now work the stitchery. The stitches used are: backstitch (BS), satin stitch (SS), lazy daisy (LD) and French knots (FK). The code numbers in the key are for Cosmo stranded embroidery threads but see General Techniques: Embroidery Threads for DMC alternatives. Use two strands of embroidery thread unless otherwise stated.

Tip *I like to use Roxanne's Glue Baste It to fix the appliqué shapes in position on the background. You could use pins but I don't like the way the thread always gets caught around pins. Being a soccer mum, I love to take my sewing whilst I watch the boys training and I never used to know what to do with the pins when I took them out. Using glue means the problem is solved!*

seven Once all the stitching has been completed gently press your work and stitch the buttons in place.

Framing the Work

eight Trim the design down, allowing sufficient excess fabric to suit your frame type. Cut a piece of cotton wadding (batting) the same size as the wooden insert from your frame. Use a hot glue gun to glue the wadding to the wooden insert. Centre the design over the wadding-covered insert and take the fabric over the edge of the insert to the back of the frame and glue in place all round. Put into the frame and enjoy.

The picture looks just as pretty in a natural wood frame, or you could paint the frame any colour you wish to complement your fabrics and threads.

Key for Threads and Stitches

Cosmo 235 pink

Roses (start in centre with FK and then BS)

Dots around daisies (FKs in groups of three)

Cosmo 312 dark brown

Tree trunk and branches (BS)

Rose bush stems (BS)

Line of ground above and below ribbon (BS)

Curly vine attached to daisies (BS)

Cosmo 364 cream

Detached petals around daisies, single strand (LD)

Dots in sky (FK)

Cosmo 575 gold

Daisy centres (fill with FKs)

Cosmo 734 blue

Blossom in tree (FKs in groups of three)

Cosmo 763 light mauve

Daisy petals (SS)

Cosmo 895 charcoal

Nesting holes in birdhouses (SS)

Perches on taller birdhouse (SS)

Heart string hanging from tree (BS)

Bird's legs (BS)

Cosmo 925 green

Leaves on tree (LD)

Leaves on rose bush (LD)

Leaves on curly vine (LD)

 Wise Mr Owl with his powerful beak waits until dark before he comes out hoot hoot hoot hoot

Garden Delights Table Centre

After months of bare trees and little colour in the garden the joy that heralds the arrival of spring brings a song to the birds and gives the bees a buzz. I have tried to capture the prettiness that is spring in this table centrepiece by using some of my favourite spring flowers and garden objects.

Finished size: 20in (51cm) diameter approximately.

What You Will Need

❀ 22in (56cm) x width of fabric of dark mushroom print for scalloped border and backing

❀ Fat quarter of light grey floral for appliqué/stitchery background

❀ 5in (12.7cm) square of mauve print for centre circle appliqué

❀ 3in x 6in (7.6cm x 15.2cm) of brown print for beehives

❀ 2in x 3in (5cm x 7.6cm) of dark teal print for beehive bases

❀ 4in (10.2cm) square of dusky pink print for birdbaths

❀ 2in x 4in (5cm x 10.2cm) of blue print for birdhouse

❀ 2in x 3in (5cm x 7.6cm) of blue stripe for birdhouse roofs

❀ 4in (10.2cm) square of creamy white wool felt for fence posts

❀ Cosmo stranded embroidery threads: 235 pink, 245 red, 312 dark brown, 364 cream, 368 pale brown, 575 gold, 734 blue, 763 light mauve, 895 charcoal and 925 green (see General Techniques: Embroidery Threads for DMC)

❀ Two bee buttons (see Suppliers)

❀ Fusible web

❀ 22in (55cm) square of stitchery stabilizer (optional)

❀ 22in (55cm) square of lightweight iron-on pellon

❀ Light box (optional)

❀ Fine-tipped fabric marking pen

❀ Roxanne's Glue Baste It ™ (optional)

Transferring the Stitchery Design

one Use the templates provided: half of the design is given in three parts. Copy Part 1, Part 2 and Part 3 and join them at the red dashed lines. Copy them all again for the other half of the design and join together into one large pattern.

two Fold your stitchery background fabric as shown in Fig 1 and lightly press the folds. Open out the folded background fabric (Fig 2). The creased lines will help to centre the design on the background fabric. Using a light source such as a light box or window, centre the background fabric right side up over the pattern, and use a fine-tipped fabric marking pen to carefully trace all the stitchery lines.

Fig 1

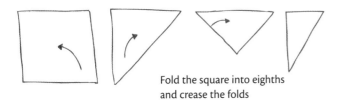

Fold the square into eighths and crease the folds

Fig 2

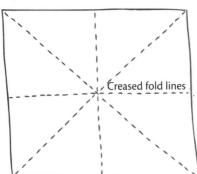

Creased fold lines

three If using an iron-on stitchery stabilizer, iron it on before starting the stitching to avoid thread shadows from showing through on the front of the work. Place the shiny side of the stabilizer on to the wrong side of your fabric and follow the manufacturer's instructions to bond it in place.

Working the Appliqué

four Using your favourite method of appliqué, prepare the shapes – beehive, beehive base, birdhouse, roof, birdbath and stand. For the centre circle draw a 4½in (11.4cm) diameter circle for a template. See General Techniques: Appliqué Methods. If using needle-turn appliqué (as I did for all pieces except for the wool fence posts) you will need to add seam allowance to the shapes. I made paper templates for the appliqué shapes and drew around the templates onto the wrong side of my fabrics. I cut the pieces out, adding a small seam allowance, and then turned the seam allowance under all round.

five Using the picture as a guide, position the appliqué shapes (a light box makes this easier). Place the pattern sheet onto the light box and position the background fabric on top. You can usually see through the fabric well enough to position the appliqué shapes. Glue baste or pin the appliqué shapes in place.

Tip When using traditional appliqué, I use a basting glue to fix the shapes in position on the background. Roxanne's Glue Baste It ™ has a small tube through which tiny drops of glue emerge, allowing for fine placement of the glue. You could use pins but thread can get caught around the pins during sewing.

Key for Threads and Stitches

Cosmo 235 pink
Daisy petals (SS)
Hollyhock (BKS in a circle)

Cosmo 245 red
Hearts on beehive doors (SS)

Cosmo 312 dark brown
Vine around centre circle (BS)
Flower stems (BS)

Cosmo 364 cream
Tiny loose petals around daisies (DLD)
Tiny loose petals around blue flowers (DLD)
Petal detail on vine daisies (LS)

Cosmo 368 pale brown
Leaves of daffodils (BS and RS)
Stems of daffodils (BS)

Cosmo 575 gold
Daffodils (BS)

Centres of daffodils (SS)
Centres of hollyhocks (FK)
Centre of blue daisies (fill with FKs)
Centre of tiny blue flowers (FK)
Alternating stripes on bees (SS)

Cosmo 734 blue
Daisy petals on vine (BS)
Birds (BS)
Bird wings (BS)
Little flowers on ground (LD)

Cosmo 763 light mauve
Hollyhocks (BKS in a circle)
Single daisies near hollyhocks (SS)

Cosmo 895 charcoal
Fence wire (BS)
Nails on fence (FK)
Alternating stripes on bees (SS)
Bee wings (BS)
Bee antennas (BS and FK)
Bee trail (RS)
Bird beaks (SS)
Bird eyes (FK)
Bird legs (BS)
Birdhouse hole and perch (SS)
Detail on beehives (RS)

Cosmo 925 green
Leaves (BS)
Leaf detail (RS)
x - - x - - x around edge (CS and RS)

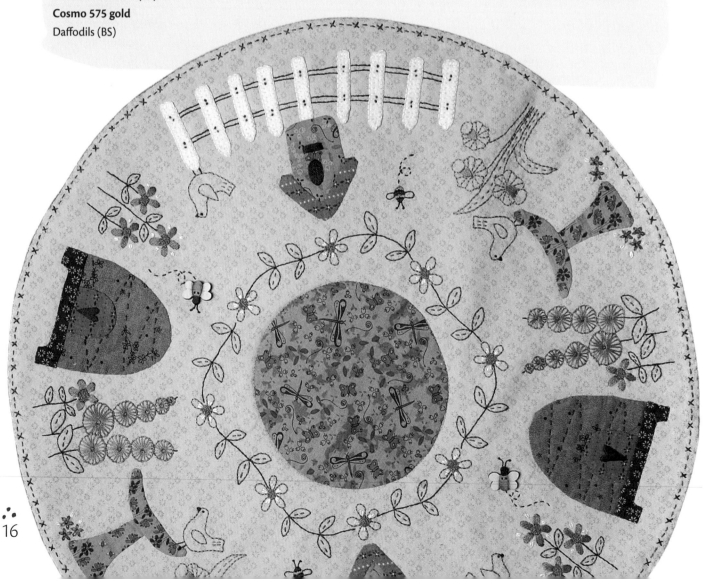

six Stitch the appliqué shapes in position using a blind hem stitch and a thread to match the background fabric so it doesn't show.

seven Back the creamy white wool felt with fusible web for the fence posts and use the template to cut out eighteen posts. Position them between the marked stitchery lines of the fence and fuse into place.

Working the Stitchery

eight Now work the stitchery. The stitches used are: backstitch (BS), blanket stitch (BKS), satin stitch (SS), cross stitch (CS), running stitch (RS), detached lazy daisy (DLD), lazy daisy (LD) long stitch (LS) and French knots (FK). The code numbers in the key are for Cosmo stranded embroidery threads but see General Techniques: Embroidery Threads for DMC alternatives. Use two strands of embroidery thread unless otherwise stated. Once all the stitching has been completed, gently press your work.

Making the Scalloped-Edge Backing

nine Cut the dark mushroom print in half, each piece about 21¾in x 22in (55cm x 56cm). Fold one piece into eighths as shown in Fig 3 and press to crease. Cut out the template for the scalloped edge from paper – this template is one eighth of the whole design. Working on a flat surface and with the *wrong side* of the fabric facing upwards, place the paper template on one of the eighth segments, making sure the point is in the centre and the edges of the template line up with the creased lines. Using a suitable fabric marking pen, draw around the scalloped top edge.

ten Flip/reverse the template and position it in the next eighth segment and draw around the top edge again (Fig 4). Flip/reverse the template, move it to the next segment and draw the line again. Repeat until all the segments have been done. Carefully press the folds out of the fabric.

Fig 3

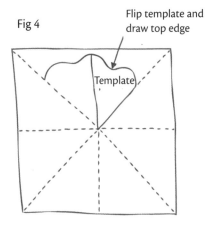

Draw line on top edge of scallop — Template

Fig 4

Flip template and draw top edge

Template

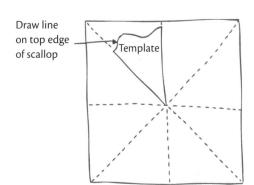

eleven Following the manufacturer's instructions bond the pellon on to the wrong side of the second piece of dark mushroom print. Place both dark mushroom print pieces right sides together, keeping the piece with the drawn lines on top. Pin the two layers together to prevent movement. Machine stitch on the drawn lines around the entire shape, to join the pieces together. Cut out about ¼in (6mm) beyond the drawn line (Fig 5).

Fig 5

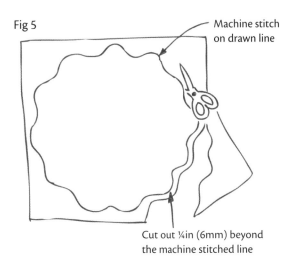

Machine stitch on drawn line

Cut out ¼in (6mm) beyond the machine stitched line

twelve Clip the seam allowance – this will help make the curves look smooth when you turn the piece to the right side. Carefully cut a short slit about 4in (10.2cm) long through just *one layer* of the dark mushroom print. Turn the work right side out through the slit. Wriggle the scallops so they sit nicely and then press.

thirteen Centre the stitchery/appliqué on top of the scalloped backing, covering the slit, and pin in place. Stitch in place all round using a blind hem stitch.

fourteen I machine quilted to hold the layers together. I stitched in the ditch around the centre circle and then around the appliqué/stitchery circle. To add the finishing touches I added a row of machine stitching about ¼in (6mm) from the scalloped edge. Stitch the buttons in place to finish.

Fig 6

Machine sewn line

Cut edge

Clip around edge

Fig 7

Cut slit through just one fabric layer

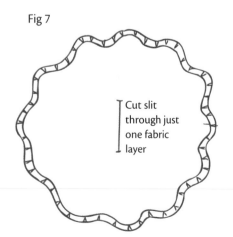

Dreaming Tree Journal

This delightful fabric-covered journal combines stitchery, English paper piecing and one of my specially designed hand-painted rabbit buttons. Miniature hexagons bring a three-dimensional feel to the hill that the dreaming tree stands on. Use this journal to record your hopes, dreams and wishes – or just the shopping list!

Finished size: 7in x 8in (19cm x 21cm) (excluding journal).

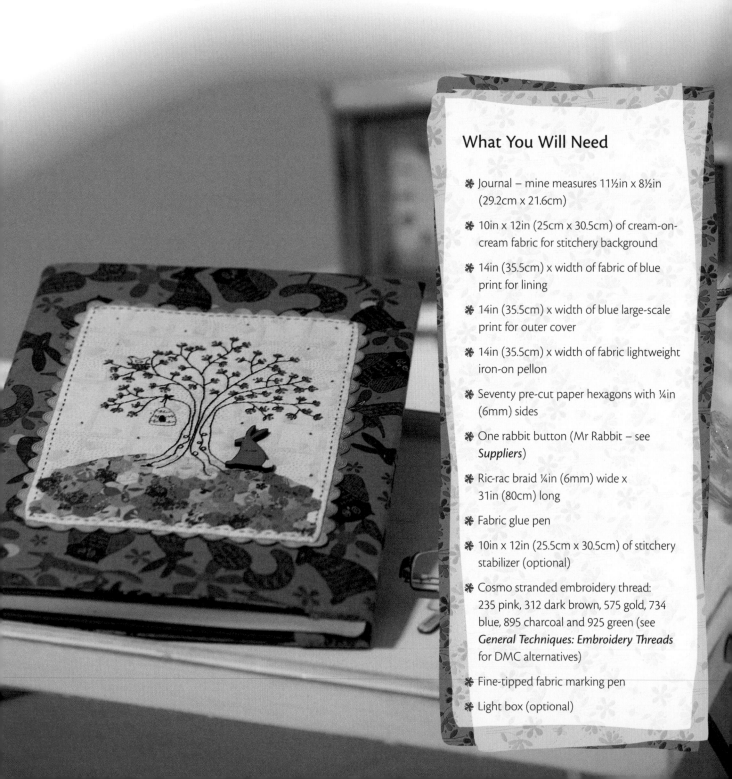

What You Will Need

❋ Journal – mine measures 11½in x 8½in (29.2cm x 21.6cm)

❋ 10in x 12in (25cm x 30.5cm) of cream-on-cream fabric for stitchery background

❋ 14in (35.5cm) x width of fabric of blue print for lining

❋ 14in (35.5cm) x width of blue large-scale print for outer cover

❋ 14in (35.5cm) x width of fabric lightweight iron-on pellon

❋ Seventy pre-cut paper hexagons with ¼in (6mm) sides

❋ One rabbit button (Mr Rabbit – see *Suppliers*)

❋ Ric-rac braid ¼in (6mm) wide x 31in (80cm) long

❋ Fabric glue pen

❋ 10in x 12in (25.5cm x 30.5cm) of stitchery stabilizer (optional)

❋ Cosmo stranded embroidery thread: 235 pink, 312 dark brown, 575 gold, 734 blue, 895 charcoal and 925 green (see *General Techniques: Embroidery Threads* for DMC alternatives)

❋ Fine-tipped fabric marking pen

❋ Light box (optional)

Making the Hexagon Hill

one Use the hexagon template provided to make a template from template plastic (seam allowance already included) and use it to cut about seventy hexagons from the assorted coordinating prints. Centre a pre-cut ¼in (6mm) hexagon on the wrong side of the fabric and either tack (baste) in place or use a glue pen (Fig 1).

Fig 1

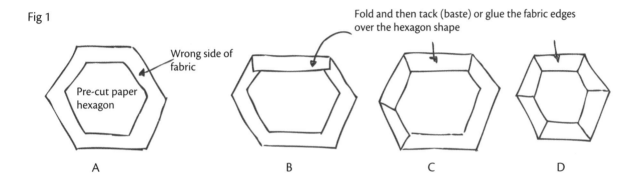

Fold and then tack (baste) or glue the fabric edges over the hexagon shape

Wrong side of fabric

Pre-cut paper hexagon

A   B   C   D

two Using the hexagon hill template as a guide for size, arrange the hexagons in rows, randomly placing the different colours.

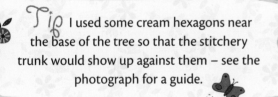

Tip I used some cream hexagons near the base of the tree so that the stitchery trunk would show up against them – see the photograph for a guide.

three Once you are happy with the fabric arrangement, stitch the hexagons together row by row (Fig 2). Place two hexagons right sides together and stitch together along the side. Repeat all along the row. Now sew all the rows together, matching the hexagon shapes neatly. Remove the papers and press the work gently.

Fig 2

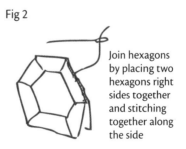

Join hexagons by placing two hexagons right sides together and stitching together along the side

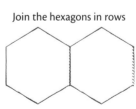

Join the hexagons in rows

Tip If you find it hard to remove the papers from the hexagons due to their tiny size then use the point of a satay or cocktail stick to carefully separate the fabric from the paper.

Key for Threads and Stitches

Cosmo 235 pink
Tree blossom (FKs in groups of 3)

Cosmo 312 dark brown
Tree trunk and branches (BS)

Cosmo 575 gold
Beehive (BS)

Cosmo 734 blue
Bird in nest (BS)
Xs in corners of outer border (CS)
- - - on outer border (RS)

Cosmo 895 charcoal
String holding beehive (BS)
Hole on beehive (SS)
Bird's nest (BS)
Bird's eye (FK)

Cosmo 925 green
Leaves on tree (DLD)

four Make a template for the hill. Place the template on the wrong side of the joined hexagons, lining up the bottom of the template with the lower row of hexagons. I kept the side and bottom hexagons as full hexagons and only cut the top curve of the hill to shape. Cut the top curve of the hill ¼in (6mm) beyond the template, turn under, tack (baste) and press. Position the hill and stitch in place with a blind hem stitch.

Working the Stitchery

five Now work the stitchery. The stitches used are: backstitch (BS), satin stitch (SS), cross stitch (CS), detached lazy daisy (DLD), running stitch (RS) and French knots (FK). The code numbers in the key are for Cosmo stranded embroidery threads but see General Techniques: Embroidery Threads for DMC alternatives. Use two strands of embroidery thread unless otherwise stated.

rabbits love lettuce and carrots
little fluffy rabbits so soft and sweet
hop hop goes the rabbit
hop hop

six When all the stitching has been completed, press your work. Trim the stitchery down to 7¾in (19.7cm) wide x 8½in (21.6cm) high. Turn about ¼in (6mm) to the wrong side, tack (baste) in place and then press.

Making the Journal Cover

seven To cover a journal with a front cover measuring 11½in x 8½in (29.2cm x 21.6cm), cut a piece 12¼in x 23in (31.1cm x 58.4cm) each from the large blue print, the iron-on pellon and lining fabric. Following the manufacturer's instructions, bond the iron-on pellon to the wrong side of the large blue print.

eight To make the cover, place the journal exterior fabric and the lining fabric right sides together and stitch around edge using ¼in (6mm) seam allowance. Leave a small opening about 3in (7.6cm) at the bottom (Fig 3). Clip the corners and turn right side out. Press lightly, making sure that none of the lining fabric can be seen from the front.

Fig 3

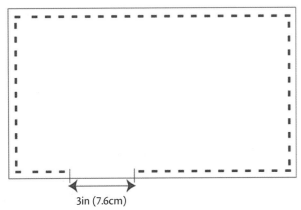

3in (7.6cm)

nine Lay the journal cover out on a flat work surface, lining side up. Put the open journal on the fabric cover and measure the turn-back required for the side flaps – remember to allow for spine of the book. Fold in the flaps on both sides and hand stitch in place (Fig 4).

Fig 4

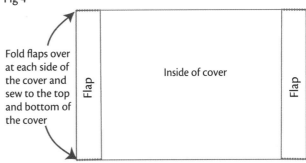

Fold flaps over at each side of the cover and sew to the top and bottom of the cover

Flap | Inside of cover | Flap

ten Put the cover on the journal to find the centre of the front cover. Position the stitchery and pin in place. Remove the cover from the book. Place the ric-rac just under the edge of the stitchery and pin the layers together before stitching in place. Stitch on the rabbit button and then slip the cover onto your journal. Now have fun using it!

23

Hexagon Handbag

This stylish hexagon bag, with its leather-look bag flap and strap, will be sure to make heads turn. It's big enough to carry the essentials without looking like an overnight bag.

Finished size: 8½in x 11in (21.6cm x 28cm) approximately.

What You Will Need

❋ 2in x 11in (5cm x 28cm) each of ten assorted fabrics for hexagons

❋ 10in (25cm) square of tone-on tone blue print for bottom of bag

❋ 10in (25cm) square of blue floral for backing

❋ 10in x 20in (25cm x 51cm) of cream print for bag lining

❋ 1½in (3.8cm) wide x width of fabric tone-on-tone blue floral for binding

❋ 22in x 2in (59cm x 5cm) lightweight iron-on pellon

❋ Fifty pre-cut paper hexagons with ¾in (2cm) sides

❋ One faux leather bag flap and straps, includes two swivel hooks and magnetic clasp (see Suppliers)

❋ Clamp/pin holder, to assist in stitching bag flap (optional) (see Suppliers)

❋ Strong thread to match bag flap

❋ Masking tape 1in (2.5cm) wide

❋ Template plastic

❋ Fabric glue pen

Making the Hexagon Patchwork

one Use the large hexagon template provided to make a template from template plastic (seam allowance already included) and use it to cut about fifty hexagons from the ten assorted coordinating prints. Centre a pre-cut paper hexagon on the wrong side of the fabric and either tack (baste) in place or use a glue pen (Fig 1). Repeat for all the hexagons.

Fig 1

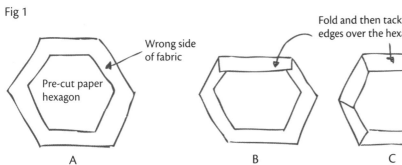

Wrong side of fabric

Pre-cut paper hexagon

Fold and then tack (baste) or glue the fabric edges over the hexagon shape

A   B   C   D

two Arrange the hexagons in a random arrangement to cover an area 8in x 10½in. Stitch the hexagons together in rows (Fig 2). Place two hexagons right sides together and stitch together along the side. Repeat all along the row. Now sew the rows together, matching hexagon shapes neatly. Remove the papers once all the hexagons are joined and press the work gently.

Fig 2

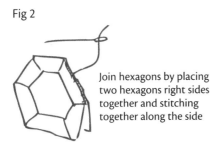

Join hexagons by placing two hexagons right sides together and stitching together along the side

Join the hexagons in rows

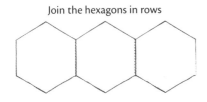

Preparing the Bag Pieces

three Preparing the following pieces of fabric for the bag (see also Fig 3).

Two pieces (A) 3½in x 10in (8.9cm x 25.4cm) from tone-on-tone blue print (one for bag front and one for bag back).

One piece (B) 7½in x 10in (19cm x 25.4cm) cut from the hexagon patchwork (for front of bag). Keeping the natural hexagon shape for the bottom of the piece, measure 7¾in (19.7cm) from the bottom point of the hexagons and cut straight at the top.

One piece 7½in x 10in (19cm x 25.4cm) from blue floral (for back of bag).

Two pieces (C) 1in x 10in (2.5cm x 25.4cm) from tone-on-tone blue print (one for bag front and one for bag back).

25

four For the front of the bag, join piece B and C together as shown in Fig 3 and press the seam. Appliqué the hexagons at the bottom of piece B, to piece A. For the back of the bag join the 7½in x 10in (19cm x 25.4cm) blue floral piece to the remaining pieces A and C.

Fig 3

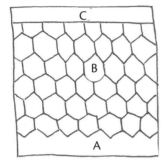

Fig 4   Diagonal grid quilting

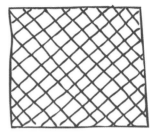

Fig 5

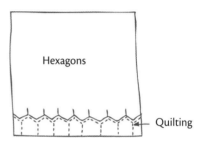

Quilting the Bag

five Bond the pellon to the wrong side of both the back and front bag pieces to stiffen and stabilize the fabrics. To quilt the back of the bag, place a strip of 1in (2.5cm) wide masking tape at a 45-degree angle on the right side of the fabric and using this as a guide, machine quilt either side of the tape. Move the tape across the surface of the fabric and quilt again. Repeat this all across the fabric. Use the tape in the same way to quilt grid lines in the opposite direction (Fig 4). I did very limited quilting on the bag front, just echoing the hexagon shapes on fabric piece A (Fig 5).

six Once the quilting has been completed trim both these pieces down to 8in (21cm) at the top x 9½in (24.1cm) at the bottom (Fig 6). Centre the magnetic clasp 2¾in (7cm) down from top edge of the bag front (Fig 7).

the naughty red fox visits my garden, he likes to hide in the bushes where he knows its safe. bark bark bark

Fig 6

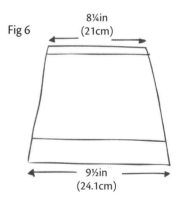

Fig 7

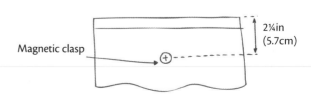

Magnetic clasp

Making the Strap Loops

seven Cut two 1in x 1½in (2.5cm x 3.8cm) pieces from the tone-on-tone blue floral. Press in ¼in (6mm) down both sides of the length. Fold the strap in half along the length, press and machine stitch. Fold each loop in half.

Putting the Bag Together

eight Place the quilted bag back and front wrong sides together, and pin together matching the side seams. Stitch the bottom seam and the side seams. To make a flat bottom to the bag, fold as shown in Fig 8 and machine stitch across the corner on both sides.

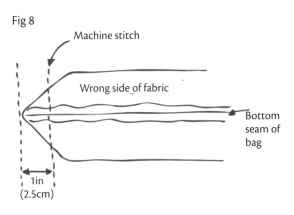

Fig 8

Machine stitch

Wrong side of fabric

Bottom seam of bag

1in (2.5cm)

nine Sew the lining pieces together in the same way as you did for the bag outer. With wrong sides together place the lining inside the bag outer. Match the side seams and pin the top edge. Centre a bag loop on both side seams and pin in place, making sure they are facing down so they don't get stitched in the wrong position (Fig 9).

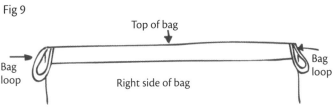

Fig 9

Top of bag

Bag loop

Right side of bag

Bag loop

ten To bind the bag, take the 1½in (3.8cm) wide tone-on-tone blue floral strip and press one long edge in about ¼in (6mm). Bind the top edge of the bag. Pin the faux leather bag flap in position on the back of the bag. Using strong thread and backstitch, stitch through the pre-punched holes on the faux leather bag flap (Fig 10), securing it to the bag. Attach the bag straps to finish.

Fig 10

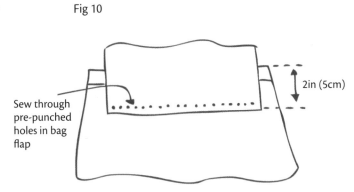

Sew through pre-punched holes in bag flap

2in (5cm)

Night Owl Purse

Stitch this sweet owl purse for the perfect place to keep your make-up, coins, key or other handbag items. Tiny yoyos add dimension to this project. Why not stitch a charm too, to decorate your purse?

Finished size: 4¼in x 2½in (10.8cm x 6.3cm) approximately.

What You Will Need

* 6in (15.2cm) square of cream print for stitchery background

* 6in (15.2cm) square of blue floral print for back of purse

* 8in x 6in (20.3cm x 15.2cm) of print fabric for lining

* Three 1½in (3.8cm) squares each of three assorted fabrics for yoyos

* 11in (28cm) square of dark blue print for bias binding

* 6in (15.2cm) square of stitchery stabilizer (optional)

* 8in x 6in (20.3cm x 15.2cm) of lightweight iron-on pellon

* Cosmo stranded embroidery thread: 312 dark brown, 364 cream, 368 light brown, 734 blue, 895 charcoal and 925 green (see General Techniques: Embroidery Threads for DMC alternatives)

* Antique gold zip (zipper) 5in (12.7cm) long

* Fine-tipped fabric marking pen

* Masking tape ½in (1.3cm) wide

* Template plastic

* Light box (optional)

Making the Bias Binding

one Using the dark blue square make 20in (51cm) of bias binding – see General Techniques. Put aside for later.

Making the Yoyos

two Using the circle template provided, cut a circle from template plastic (seam allowance included in template). Make one yoyo from each of the three fabrics.

Transferring the Stitchery Design

three Using the template and light source, centre the cream background fabric right side up over the pattern. Use a fabric pen to trace the stitchery lines. If using iron-on stabilizer, iron it on before working the stitchery.

Working the Stitchery

four The stitches used are: backstitch (BS), satin stitch (SS), long stitch (LS), running stitch (RS) and French knots (FK). Code numbers are for Cosmo stranded embroidery threads but you could use DMC alternatives. Use two strands unless otherwise stated. Press the finished stitching. Stitch the yoyo in place.

Making Up the Purse

five From template plastic make templates A and B (seam allowances are included). Trace template A onto the cream fabric. Cut out on the line. Trace template B on the blue print. Cut out on the line. Sew A and B right sides together along the straight edge (Fig 1).

Fig 1
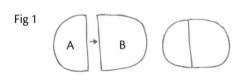

six Bond the pellon to the wrong side of the lining piece. Put the stitched purse outer right side up on the pellon and machine quilt a diagonal grid pattern (Fig 2). Use the masking tape as a guide, quilting either side of the tape and moving it across the fabric. Trim the pellon and lining to the same size as the stitched purse outer.

Fig 2
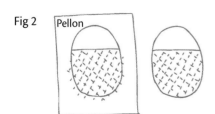

Key for Threads and Stitches

Cosmo 312 dark brown
Branch (BS)

Cosmo 364 cream
Dots on owl chest (FK)

Cosmo 368 pale brown
Owl (BS)
Owl wing markings (RS)

Cosmo 734 blue
Stars (1 strand LS)

Cosmo 895 charcoal
Outline owl eye (BS)
Owl eye (FK)
Owl beak (SS)
Owl feet (LS)

Cosmo 925 green
Leaves (BS)
Veins on leaves (RS)

seven Use the binding to bind around the edge of the oval. With right sides together and matching the top curve of the purse, check the zip length and pin mark where it starts and stops (Fig 3). Hand stitch the side of the purse together. Repeat for other side. Backstitch the zip into place, first on one side and then the other (Fig 4). To neaten inside of purse, stitch the selvedge side of the zip to the lining of the purse.

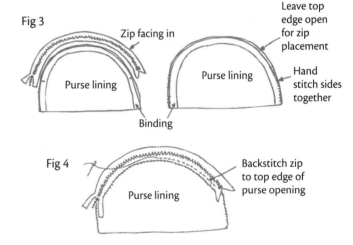

Fig 3

Zip facing in

Leave top edge open for zip placement

Purse lining

Purse lining

Hand stitch sides together

Binding

Fig 4

Purse lining

Backstitch zip to top edge of purse opening

eight To make a flat bottom to the purse, fold and machine stitch across the corner on both sides (Fig 5). Turn through to the right side and enjoy!

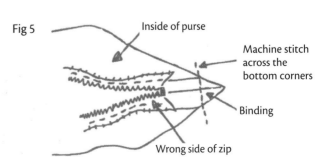

Fig 5

Inside of purse

Machine stitch across the bottom corners

Binding

Wrong side of zip

Night and Day Charms

These lovely stitched charms look great on the end of a special key, attached to your scissors or on the front of your hexagon bag. Choose to stitch a sweet owl for a night motif or a butterfly for day.

Finished size: 2in (5cm) diameter approximately.

What You Will Need (for one charm)

* 5in (12.7cm) square of cream print for stitchery background

* 5in (12.7cm) square of blue or pink floral for backing

* 5in (12.7cm) square of stitchery stabilizer (optional)

* Cosmo stranded embroidery threads: 235 pink, 312 dark brown, 364 cream, 734 blue, 763 light mauve, 895 charcoal and 925 dark green (see General Techniques: Embroidery Threads for DMC alternatives)

* Two plastic domes 2in (5cm) diameter

* Fine-tipped fabric marking pen

* One antique gold key

* Craft glue, clear quick-drying

Transferring the Design

one Using the template provided and a light source such as a light box or window, centre the cream background fabric right side up over the pattern. Use a fabric pen to carefully trace the stitchery lines.

two If using an iron-on stitchery stabilizer, iron it on before starting the stitching to avoid thread shadows on the front of the work. Place the shiny side of the stabilizer on to the wrong side of your fabric and follow the manufacturer's instructions to bond it in place.

Working the Stitchery

three Work the stitchery following the information on the stitcheries templates. The stitches used are: backstitch (BS), satin stitch (SS), running stitch (RS), lazy daisy (LD), long stitch (LS) and French knots (FK). Code numbers in the key are for Cosmo stranded embroidery threads but see General Techniques: Embroidery Threads for DMC alternatives. Use two strands of embroidery thread.

four When stitching is completed, press gently. Cut out on the outside line (shown in blue on the stitcheries templates). Using a double strand of sewing cotton, work a row of running stitches around the edge of the circle about ⅛in (3mm) in from the edge. Place the plastic dome to the wrong side of the stitched circle and gently pull on the running stitches to gather the circle tightly around the dome. Finish off the thread. Cut another circle from print fabric and cover the second dome.

Making the Tassel and Cord

five To make the tassel cut a piece of card 1¼in (3.2cm) wide. Take a six-stranded length of two different colours of stranded embroidery threads and wrap around the card ten times – start counting from the bottom of card. Carefully slide the threads off the card.

six To make the cord, cut a 20in (50cm) six-stranded length of two colours and twist them together until the cord wants to double back on itself, but don't let it yet! Thread the twisted cord through the top loop of the tassel, centre the tassel on the cord and now let the cord double back on itself, holding onto the ends while it twists. Tie a small knot at the end to secure the twisted cord. Cut through the bottom loops of the tassel. Take a

short length of six-stranded thread and wrap it around tassel several times about ¼in (6mm) from the top loop. Secure with a knot and put the thread ends out of sight.

Assembling the Stitched Charm

seven Take one of the plastic domes and glue the tied end of the cord into the centre of the wrong side, placing the glue just inside the edge. Glue the two domes together, making sure that the twisted cord comes out at the centre top. Using two strands of your favourite colour thread, work herringbone stitch to cover the join of the two domes, all the way around the edge.

Fig 1

Making the Yoyos

eight Using the circular template provided make three yoyos from three different prints – see General Techniques: Making Yoyos. Glue the yoyos in position to finish.

Spring Flower Quilt

This fresh spring flower quilt is quick and fun to make. The subtle mauves, blues and pinks combine to give a feminine look that no girl can resist. Blanket stitch appliqué and easy nine-patch blocks make this project suitable for all quilters.

Finished size: 40in x 52in (101cm x 132cm) approximately.

What You Will Need

❋ 5in x width of fabric each of twelve assorted coordinating prints for nine-patch blocks and corner triangles

❋ 19½in (49.5cm) x width of fabric of cream-on-cream print for flower background

❋ 6in (15.2cm) x width of fabric of dark mauve floral for inner border

❋ 22½in (57cm) x width of fabric of blue feature print for outer border

❋ 15in (15.2cm) x width of fabric of mauve print for appliqué flowers

❋ 2in (5cm) x width of fabric of dark teal print for flower centres

❋ Dusky pink stripe fabric for binding ½yd/m (¾yd/m if cut on the bias)

❋ Stranded embroidery thread in charcoal for blanket stitch

❋ Fusible web

❋ Wadding (batting) 48in x 60in (122cm x 152.5cm) approximately

❋ Backing fabric 48in x 60in (122cm x 152.5cm) approximately

❋ Fine-tipped fabric marking pen

Making the Nine-Patch Blocks

one From the twelve coordinating fabrics cut 230 squares each 2½in (6.3cm). Choose nine of the squares at random and join to make one nine-patch block as shown in Fig 1A–C. Press the seam well. The finished block size should be 6½in (16.5cm) including seam allowance Make eighteen blocks like this in total.

Fig 1

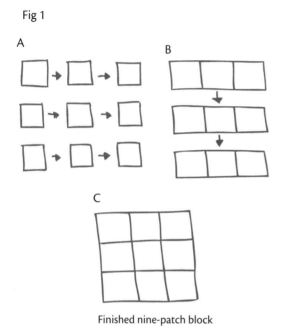

Finished nine-patch block

Making the Snowball Blocks

two From cream-on-cream background print cut seventeen 6½in (16.5cm) squares. To make a snowball block take one of these cream squares and four of the assorted coordinating print 2½in (6.3cm) squares. On the wrong side of the fabric use a fine-tipped fabric pen to draw a line diagonally on all four of the 2½in (6.3cm) squares (Fig 2A). With right sides together, place a 2½in (6.3cm) square on each corner of the 6½in (16.5cm) background square. Stitch on the drawn line and then press the triangles outwards (Fig 2B). Make seventeen snowball blocks in total.

Joining the Blocks

three Take the eighteen nine-patch blocks and the seventeen snowball blocks and arrange them alternately in seven rows, as shown in Fig 3. Using a ¼in (6mm) seam allowance, sew the blocks together in rows, matching seams carefully. Press the seams. Now sew the rows together, matching seams. Press the quilt top.

Fig 3

Fig 2

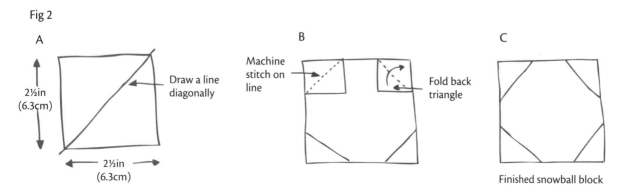

A
2½in (6.3cm)
2½in (6.3cm)
Draw a line diagonally

B
Machine stitch on line
Fold back triangle

C
Finished snowball block

Adding the Inner Border

four From the dark mauve floral cut two strips each 1½in x 42½in (3.8cm x 108cm) for the side borders and two strips each 1½in x 32½in (3.8cm x 82.5cm) for the top and bottom borders. Join the side borders to the quilt first and press seams. Now sew on the top and bottom borders (Fig 4).

Working the Appliqué

six Using the templates provided and your favourite method of appliqué (see General Techniques: Appliqué Methods), apply the daisy flowers and then their centres to the snowball blocks. I used a fusible web method of appliqué for my quilt with a blanket stitch edging in charcoal embroidery thread (two strands) around the flowers and their centres (see General Techniques: Embroidery Stitches).

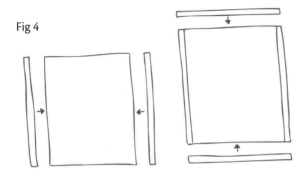

Fig 4

Adding the Outer Border

five From the blue feature print cut five strips each 4½in (11.4cm) x width of fabric and join these together to form a long length. Press seams open. From this cut two strips each 4½in x 32½in (11.4cm x 82.5cm) for the top and bottom borders and two strips each 4½in x 52½in (11.4 x 133.4cm) for the side borders. Join the top and bottom borders to the quilt first and press seams. Now sew on the side borders (Fig 5).

Fig 5

Quilting the Quilt

seven Prepare the quilt for quilting using your wadding (batting) and backing fabric. I machine quilted in the ditch between the blocks and in the seams of the individual nine-patch and snowball blocks. I also machine quilted a flower pattern within each nine-patch block. See General Techniques: Quilting.

Binding the Quilt

eight Bind the edge of the quilt to finish. For a straight-cut, double-fold binding with a starting width of 2½in (6.3cm), cut five strips of fabric across the fabric width. Join the strips together and press seams open. Fold in half along the length and press. Now refer to General Techniques: Binding.

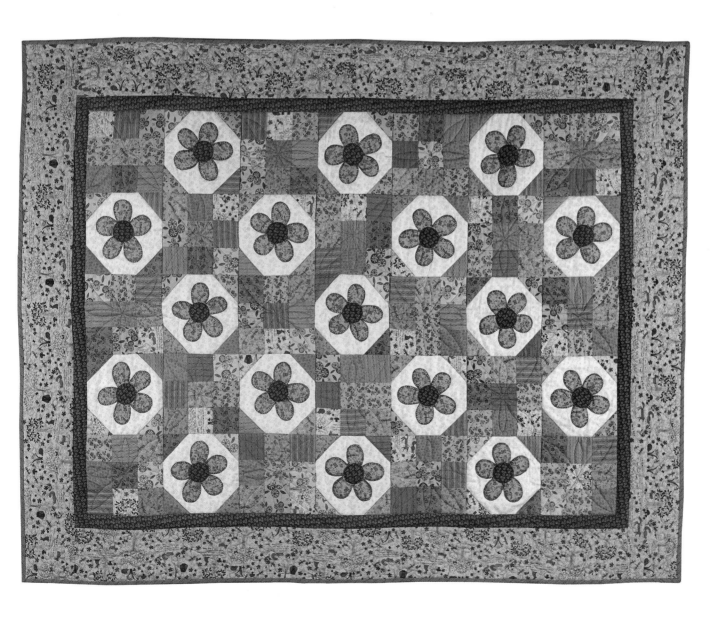

Sweet Rabbit Tea Towel

Bring a spring theme to your kitchen with this easy to make, sweetly decorated tea towel. Simple blanket stitch appliqué and a ready-made tea towel make this a quick project. Alternatively, you could have fun using the same images to decorate a child's T-shirt.

Finished size: 23in x 17in (58.4cm x 43.2cm).

What You Will Need

* One cream ready-made tea towel about 23in x 17in (58.4cm x 43.2cm)

* 1in x 17in (2.5cm x 43.2cm) of blue striped fabric for top strip of bottom border

* 2½in x 17in (6.3cm x 43.2cm) of mauve print for lower strip of bottom border

* 2in (5cm) square of soft green print for appliqué leaves

* 3in (7.6cm) square of mauve print for flower appliqué

* 1½in (3.8cm) square of blue print for flower centre

* 5½in x 7in (14cm x 18cm) of brown print for rabbits

* 2½in (6.3cm) square each of two different prints for rabbit's tails

* 17in (43.2cm) of narrow cream lace

* 2½in (6.3cm) x width of fabric of pink print for binding

* Stranded embroidery threads in green and charcoal

* One butterfly button (see Suppliers)

* Fusible web

* Fine-tipped fabric marking pen

Making the Bottom Border

one Take the 1in x 17in (2.5cm x 43.2cm) blue striped fabric and the 2½in x 17in (6.3cm x 43.2cm) mauve print and sew together to form a strip 3in x 17in (7.6cm x 43.2cm). Press the seam open.

two Press a ¼in (6mm) seam along the top edge. Align the border with the bottom edge of the tea towel and stitch in place. Stitch the lace over the seam.

Fig 1

3in (7.6cm)

17in (43.2cm)

Fig 2

Turn under ¼in (6mm) and press

Wrong side of fabric

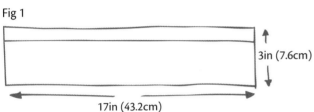

Working the Appliqué

three You can do the appliqué now or after the stitchery has been done – I do mine before. Using your favourite method of appliqué and the picture as a guide for positioning, apply the rabbits and the flower. I used a fusible web method but if you prefer a needle-turn method you will need to add seam allowances to the shapes. Refer to General Techniques: Appliqué Methods.

Working the Stitchery

four Using a suitable fabric marking pen, draw freehand the stem for the flower. Using two strands of stranded embroidery thread, stitch the stem in green chain stitch. Backstitch the rabbit's eyes in charcoal. Work green running stitch in the centre of the leaves. Work charcoal running stitch for the butterfly trail.

five Using the circle template make two yoyos from different prints – see General Techniques: Making Yoyos. Stitch them in position.

Binding the Tea Towel

six Bind the edge of the tea towel using the 2½in (6.3cm) fabric strip – see General Techniques: Binding.

Silly squirrels jumping from branch to branch playing catch me and looking for food. leap leap

leap leap

Templates

This section contains the stitchery and appliqué templates for the projects, which are all shown at full size. Templates being used for needle-turn appliqué will need to have ¼in (6mm) seam allowances added. Templates being used for fusible web appliqué will need to be reversed (flipped), unless the design is symmetrical. See General Techniques for Using Templates, Reversing Templates and Transferring Designs.

Birdhouse Blossoms Picture
Appliqué Templates
(actual size)

If using needle-turn appliqué add ¼in (6mm) seam allowance all round

If using fusible web appliqué the templates will need to be reversed

- - - - - - indicates an area that will be under another piece of appliqué

Surface stitchery to be worked on the appliqué is shown in red

Birdhouse Blossoms Picture

Stitchery Design
(actual size)

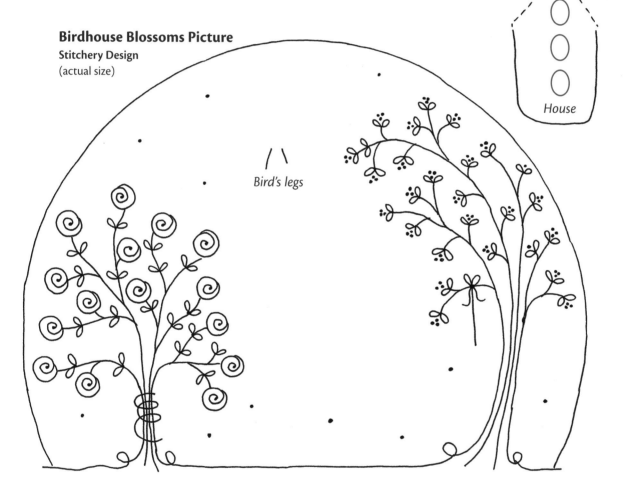

Bird's legs

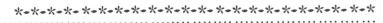

Garden Delights Table Centre
Appliqué and Surface Stitchery Templates (actual size)

If using needle-turn appliqué add ¼in (6mm) seam allowance all round
If using fusible web appliqué the templates will need to be reversed
- - - - - indicates an area that will be under another piece of appliqué
Surface stitchery to be worked on the appliqué is shown in red
Green lines indicate appliqué placement on the stitchery

Garden Delights Table Centre
Stitchery Design
(actual size)

Half the design is shown
split into Part 1, Part 2 and
Part 3. Copy and tape the
parts together, joining them
at the red dashed lines and
then copy again and rotate
for the other half

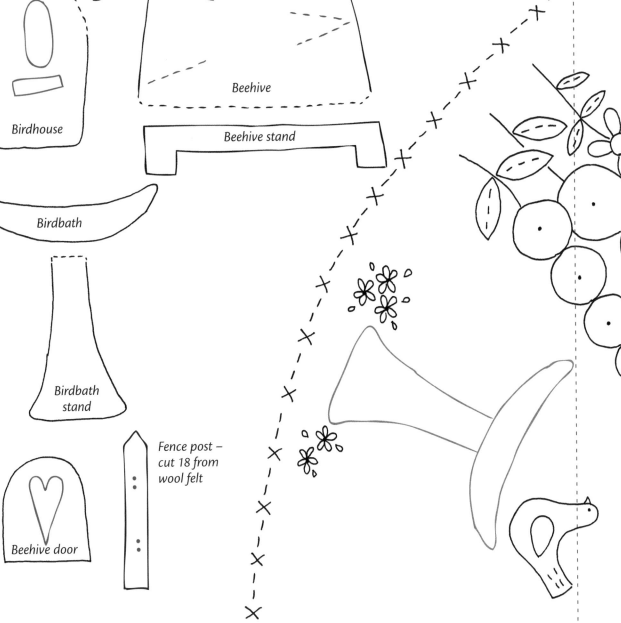

39

Part 2 of Stitchery Design

Join Part 1 to Part 2 here

Join Part 2 to Part 3 here

Bee button

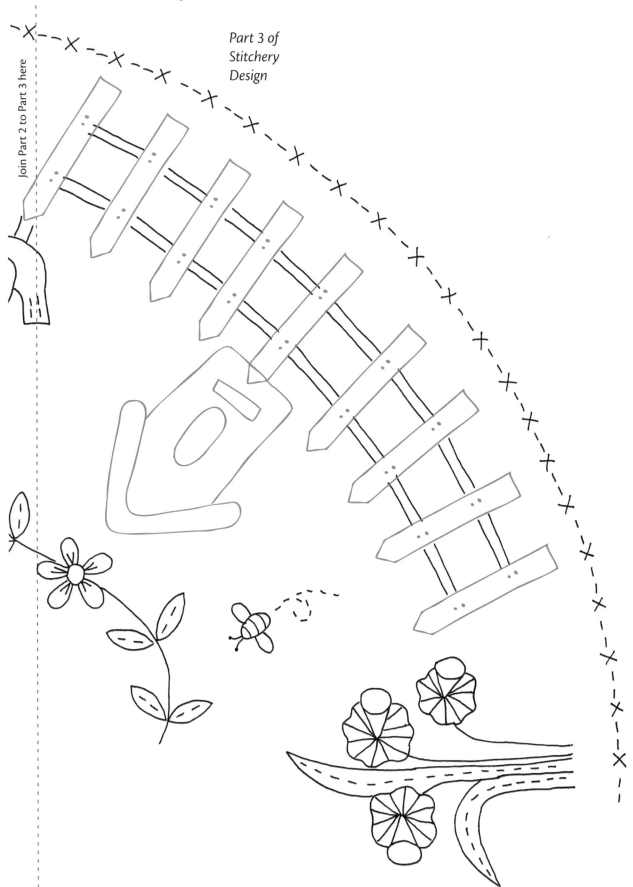

*Part 3 of
Stitchery
Design*

Join Part 2 to Part 3 here

**Garden Delights
Table Centre**

Scallop Template
One eighth of the design
(actual size)

10⅛in (25.7cm)

Dreaming Tree Journal
Stitchery Design
(actual size)

Hexagon Template
¼in (6mm) sides
(actual size)

Paper
template

Fabric template
(includes seam allowance)

Dreaming Tree Journal
Hexagon Hill Template
(actual size)

Use this as a guide for the shape
of the joined hexagons

Night Owl Purse
Stitchery Design
(actual size)

Yoyo template
(actual size)

1¾in (4.4cm) diameter
(seam allowance included)
Cut 3

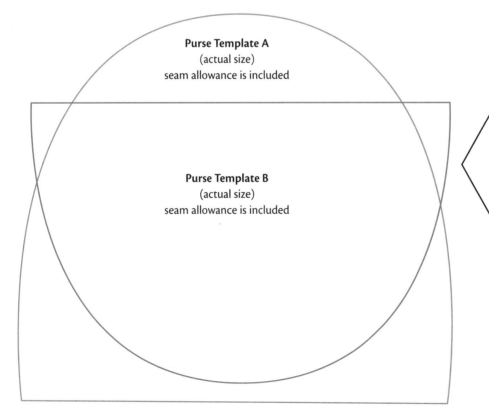

Purse Template A
(actual size)
seam allowance is included

Purse Template B
(actual size)
seam allowance is included

Hexagon Bag
Hexagon Templates
(actual size)

Fabric template
(includes seam allowance)

¾in (2cm) sides

Paper template

Night and Day Charms

Stitchery Designs
(actual size)

Threads and Stitches Key
Cosmo threads have been used – see
General Techniques: Embroidery Threads
for DMC equivalents

Backstitch (BS)
French knot (FK)
Lazy daisy stitch (LD)
Long stitch (LS)
Running stitch (RS)
Satin stitch (SS)

Yoyo template
(actual size)

1½in (3.8cm) diameter
(seam included)
Cut 3

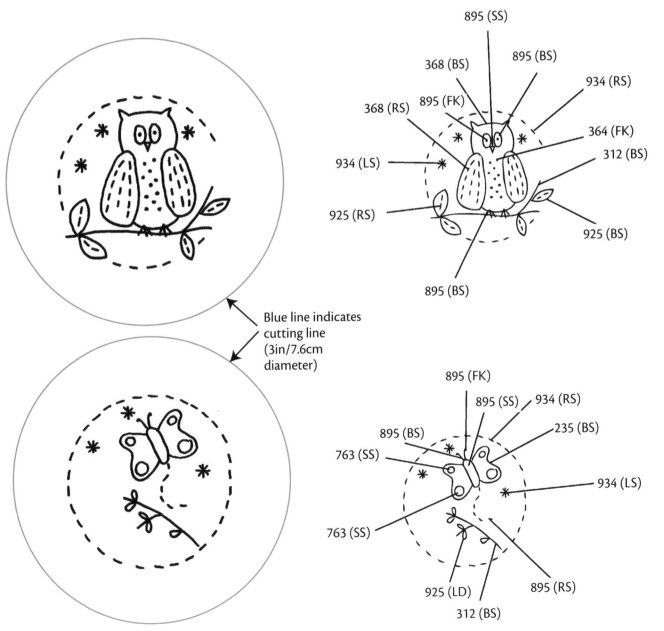

Blue line indicates
cutting line
(3in/7.6cm
diameter)

895 (SS)
895 (BS)
368 (BS)
934 (RS)
368 (RS)
895 (FK)
364 (FK)
934 (LS)
312 (BS)
925 (RS)
925 (BS)
895 (BS)

895 (FK)
895 (SS)
934 (RS)
895 (BS)
235 (BS)
763 (SS)
934 (LS)
763 (SS)
925 (LD)
895 (RS)
312 (BS)

45

Spring Flower Quilt
Appliqué Templates
(actual size)

Flower
centre
Cut 17

Flower
Cut 17

Sweet Rabbit Tea Towel
Appliqué Templates
(actual size)

Flower
Cut 1

Rabbit
Cut 1 and
1 reversed

Leaf
Cut 1

Yoyo template
(actual size)

2in (5cm) diameter
(seam allowance included)
Cut 2

Flower centre
Cut 1

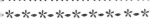

Suppliers

Coast & Country Crafts & Quilts
Barras Moor, Perranarworthal, Truro,
Cornwall TR3 7PE, UK
Tel: 01872 870478
www.coastandcountrycrafts.co.uk
For patchwork and quilting supplies

Craftime Ltd
Unit 1 Apollo Business Park, Charles Way,
Bulwell, Nottingham NG6 8RF, UK
Tel: 01159 519827
www.craftime.com
*For Lynette Anderson licensed products
(ribbons, buttons, braid and paper products)*

Little Quilt Store
924 David Low Way, Marcoola, Sunshine
Coast, QLD 4564 Australia
Tel: +61 (7) 5450 7497
Email: sales@littlequiltstore.com.au
www.littlequiltstore.com
*For Lynette's books, fabrics, buttons, paper
products, printed ribbons, frames, English
paper pieces, Cosmo threads, zips, bag flaps,
straps, clamp/pin holders and plastic domes*

Stitch Craft Create
www.stitchcraftcreate.co.uk

Lea Bye Moss Recycled Vintage Handcrafted Furniture
Greenoaks Drive, Coolum Beach,
Queensland 4573 Australia
Email: mossgoodsofdesire@hotmail.com

Lecien Corporation
Art and Hobby Division, 7F Yotsubashi
Grand Square, 1-28-3 Shinmachi Nishi-ku,
Osaka 550-0013 Japan
Tel: +81-6-4390-5516
www.lecien.co.jp/en/hobby
*For Cosmo threads and fabrics, including
those designed by Lynette Anderson*

Lynette Anderson Designs
PO Box 9314, Pacific Paradise, QLD 4564
Australia
Tel: +61 (7) 5450 7497
Email: info@lynetteandersondesigns.com.au
www.lynetteandersondesigns.com.au
For wholesale enquires and teaching info

Sandra Faye Photographer
www.sandrafayephotographer.com.au

Yankee Doodle Quilting
Elaine Wiles (machine quilting)
Email: new2@westnet.com.au

Index

About the Author

Lynette Anderson's love affair with textiles began when she was growing up in a village in Dorset, England, where her grandmother taught her to embroider and knit. Moving with her family to Australia in 1990 prompted the release of her first patchwork patterns in 1995. Her distinctive style encompasses quilts, pillow, bags and sewing accessories. Lynette also designs wooden buttons, cut to her original drawings and hand-painted locally to her specifications. In 2010 Lynette was excited to fulfil her dream of putting her designs on to fabric when she was asked to design for Lecien. Collections include 'Summertime Friends', 'Scandinavian Christmas', 'Secret Garden', 'Hollyhock Cottage', 'Happy Halloween', 'Christmas Fun' and 'Follow My Heart'. A busy year is planned for 2013 with the release of fabric collections 'Wildflower Wood', 'Candy Cane Angels' and 'Mending Fences'.

Lynette's first professionally published book, *It's Quilting Cats & Dogs*, was for David & Charles in 2010 and is filled with heart-warming designs that combine simple but stunning hand stitchery with traditional patchwork and quilting. This was followed by *Country Cottage Quilting* in March 2012, a lovely collection of projects showcasing Lynette's original and distinctive style. A charming collection of festive designs, *Stitch It For Christmas*, was published in 2012. For more about Lynette visit her blog: www.lynetteandersondesigns.typepad.com.

Acknowledgments

There are many people I would like to thank. Nireko from Lecien fabrics for her friendship and for making sure that the fabrics for this book arrived on time. Sandra, for her artistic guidance and patience during the photo shoot, and for the fabulous photos. My neighbour, who at the drop of a pin will machine quilt for me – Elaine I love the quilting you do. Val, for helping me meet my deadlines and for doing some of the embroidery – your satin stitch is the best. Lea, who loaned me the wonderful vintage meat safe, without which the front cover would not look so good.

A DAVID & CHARLES BOOK
© F&W Media International, Ltd 2013

David & Charles is an imprint of F&W Media
International, Ltd
Brunel House, Forde Close, Newton Abbot,
TQ12 4PU, UK

F&W Media International, Ltd is a subsidiary
of F+W Media, Inc
10151 Carver Road, Suite #200, Blue Ash,
OH 45242, USA

Text and Designs © Lynette Anderson 2013
Layout and Photography © F&W Media
International, Ltd 2013

First published in the UK and USA in 2013

Lynette Anderson has asserted her right to be
identified as author of this work in accordance
with the Copyright, Designs and Patents Act, 1988.

A catalogue record for this book is available from
the British Library.

ISBN-13: 978-1-4463-0317-7 paperback
ISBN-10: 1-4463-0317-9 paperback

Printed in China by RR Donnelley for:
F&W Media International, Ltd
Brunel House, Forde Close, Newton Abbot,
TQ12 4PU, UK

10 9 8 7 6 5 4 3 2 1

Acquisitions Editor: Sarah Callard
Editor: Jeni Hennah
Project Editor: Lin Clements
Art Editor: Jodie Lystor
Photographer: Sandra Faye
Senior Production Controller: Kelly Smith

F+W Media publishes high quality books on a wide
range of subjects. For more great book ideas visit:
www.stitchcraftcreate.co.uk